William Howe

British General

Colonial Leaders

Lord Baltimore
English Politician and Colonist

Benjamin Banneker
American Mathematician and Astronomer

Sir William Berkeley
Governor of Virginia

William Bradford
Governor of Plymouth Colony

Jonathan Edwards
Colonial Religious Leader

Benjamin Franklin
American Statesman, Scientist, and Writer

Anne Hutchinson
Religious Leader

Cotton Mather
Author, Clergyman, and Scholar

Increase Mather
Clergyman and Scholar

James Oglethorpe
Humanitarian and Soldier

William Penn
Founder of Democracy

Sir Walter Raleigh
English Explorer and Author

Caesar Rodney
American Patriot

John Smith
English Explorer and Colonist

Miles Standish
Plymouth Colony Leader

Peter Stuyvesant
Dutch Military Leader

George Whitefield
Clergyman and Scholar

Roger Williams
Founder of Rhode Island

John Winthrop
Politician and Statesman

John Peter Zenger
Free Press Advocate

Revolutionary War Leaders

John Adams
Second U.S. President

Samuel Adams
Patriot

Ethan Allen
Revolutionary Hero

Benedict Arnold
Traitor to the Cause

John Burgoyne
British General

George Rogers Clark
American General

Lord Cornwallis
British General

Thomas Gage
British General

King George III
English Monarch

Nathanael Greene
Military Leader

Nathan Hale
Revolutionary Hero

Alexander Hamilton
First U.S. Secretary of the Treasury

John Hancock
President of the Continental Congress

Patrick Henry
American Statesman and Speaker

William Howe
British General

John Jay
First Chief Justice of the Supreme Court

Thomas Jefferson
Author of the Declaration of Independence

John Paul Jones
Father of the U.S. Navy

Thaddeus Kosciuszko
Polish General and Patriot

Lafayette
French Freedom Fighter

James Madison
Father of the Constitution

Francis Marion
The Swamp Fox

James Monroe
American Statesman

Thomas Paine
Political Writer

Molly Pitcher
Heroine

Paul Revere
American Patriot

Betsy Ross
American Patriot

Baron Von Steuben
American General

George Washington
First U.S. President

Anthony Wayne
American General

Famous Figures of the Civil War Era

John Brown
Abolitionist

Jefferson Davis
Confederate President

Frederick Douglass
Abolitionist and Author

Stephen A. Douglas
Champion of the Union

David Farragut
Union Admiral

Ulysses S. Grant
Military Leader and President

Stonewall Jackson
Confederate General

Joseph E. Johnston
Confederate General

Robert E. Lee
Confederate General

Abraham Lincoln
Civil War President

George Gordon Meade
Union General

George McClellan
Union General

William Henry Seward
Senator and Statesman

Philip Sheridan
Union General

William Sherman
Union General

Edwin Stanton
Secretary of War

Harriet Beecher Stowe
Author of Uncle Tom's Cabin

James Ewell Brown Stuart
Confederate General

Sojourner Truth
Abolitionist, Suffragist, and Preacher

Harriet Tubman
Leader of the Underground Railroad

William Howe

British General

Bruce Adelson

Arthur M. Schlesinger, jr.
Senior Consulting Editor

Chelsea House Publishers

Philadelphia

CHELSEA HOUSE PUBLISHERS
Editor-in-Chief Sally Cheney
Director of Production Kim Shinners
Production Manager Pamela Loos
Art Director Sara Davis
Production Editor Diann Grasse

Staff for *WILLIAM HOWE*
Editor Sally Cheney
Associate Art Director Takeshi Takahashi
Series Design Keith Trego
Cover Design 21st Century Publishing and Communications, Inc.
Picture Researcher Jane Sanders
Layout 21st Century Publishing and Communications, Inc.

The Chelsea House World Wide Web address is
http://www.chelseahouse.com

First Printing
1 3 5 7 9 8 6 4 2

Library of Congress Cataloging-in-Publication Data

Adelson, Bruce.
   British General William Howe / Bruce Adelson.
      p. cm. — (Revolutionary War leaders)
   Includes bibliographical references and index.
   ISBN 0-7910-6388-7 (hc : alk. paper) — ISBN 0-7910-6389-5
   (pbk. : alk. paper)
      1. Howe, William Howe, Viscount, 1729–1814—Juvenile literature.
   2. United States—History—Revolution, 1775–1783—British forces
   —Juvenile literature. 3. Generals—Great Britain—Biography—
   Juvenile literature. [1. Howe, William Howe, Viscount, 1729–1814.
   2. Generals. 3. United States—History—Revolution, 1775–1783.]
   I. Title. II. Series.

   DA67.1.H6 A67 2001
   973.3'41'092—dc21
   [B]   2001028526

Publisher's Note: In Colonial and Revolutionary War America,
there were no standard rules for spelling, punctuation, capitaliza-
tion, or grammar. Some of the quotations that appear in the Colonial Leaders and Revolutionary War Leaders series come from
original documents and letters written during this time in history.
Original quotations reflect writing inconsistencies of the period.

Contents

As a young man, William Howe attended Eton, the well-known British preparatory school on the River Thames.

A Military Family

William Howe was destined for great things. Born on August 10, 1729, in England, he was the youngest of his parents' three sons. All three boys eventually grew up to be famous soldiers in the army and navy. Their parents were wealthy members of the English upper class. William's father, **Viscount** Howe, was a nobleman, and his mother was Maria Sophia, also a member of the English upper class, who may have been a relative of the English king, George I. Viscount, like Baron and Lord, is a title held by people called nobles. They can trace their families back hundreds of years. Many nobles are also related to the king or queen of England.

When he was about 12 years old, William was sent away from home to go to Eton, a famous preparatory school in England. Although he was not the best student at Eton, William did study hard. In 1746, after graduating from school, William entered the King's army. He was appointed as an officer in a military unit known as the "Duke of Cumberland's Light **Dragoons**."

William moved up quickly in the army. After just one year of service, he was promoted to the rank of lieutenant. By 1759, when he was 30 years old, William became a lieutenant colonel and commanded his own **regiment** of soldiers.

At that time, Great Britain was at war with France. These countries were two of the most powerful in Europe in the mid-18th century. They were also big rivals. Both had large armies and navies. They also had large colonies in the "New World," North America. France controlled part of Canada, and Great Britain had 13 colonies in what is now the United States. In 1756, Great Britain and France began fighting what later became known as the **French**

This map shows the 13 British colonies as they looked in 1775.

and Indian War or the Seven Years' War, because it lasted seven years, for control of North America.

During this war, William's oldest brother, Lord George Howe, who was an officer in the British army and also a member of **Parliament,** was killed in 1758 while fighting in New York. After George's death, his mother asked the people of Nottingham, whom George represented in Parliament, to replace him with her youngest son, William. They agreed, and William became the next Howe to be a member of Parliament. But William did not have time to enjoy his new position. He and his regiment sailed from Ireland in 1758 to join the fight against the French for the New World.

Shortly after arriving, William and his men were quickly sent into action. They defeated the French in a battle for the town of Louisburg in Canada. His troops performed so well in that battle that other British officers noticed their skill. **General** Wolfe, the commander of British troops in North America, recognized William's accomplishments when he wrote, "Our old comrade Howe is at the head of the best trained battalion in all of America."

In 1759, General Wolfe ordered William to help capture the important Canadian city of Quebec. The French controlled Quebec and had already defeated Wolfe in his first try to capture the city. But Wolfe knew that to win the war, he had to capture

Quebec. He decided to use William to lead a dangerous surprise attack.

William and 24 volunteers were supposed to climb a steep cliff and surprise the French soldiers at the top. After reaching the top and defeating the French troops there, the rest of the British army would follow Howe and battle the French for control of Quebec. But everything depended on William's success. If he were defeated, the entire attack against Quebec would probably fail.

William and his volunteers had a very difficult job. Not only was the cliff very steep, but French troops were on guard all across the top.

In the middle of the night, William and his soldiers started to climb over boulders, rocks, and logs. They moved quickly and silently through the cliff's trees and bushes. They had to be careful not to make any noise, so the French would be surprised by the attack. Slipping, sliding, and holding onto tree branches, the 25 British soldiers slowly made their way up.

Finally, the British were at the top of the cliff.

They looked around for the enemy. With dawn approaching, there was enough light for them to see the French soldiers' tents nearby. William decided to rush the tents and capture the French while they slept. Moving quickly, the soldiers surprised the enemy commander and his troops, capturing them without firing a shot, even though there were many more French soldiers than the 25 British. The French were so shocked to see the British soldiers that they did not have time to fire their weapons before being captured.

With the cliffs in British control, General Wolfe and the rest of the army followed William's lead, stormed Quebec, and defeated the French army. William's daringly successful assault was the key to the British victory in the Battle of Quebec.

Although they lost the battle, the French did not surrender. During the winter of 1759-1760, French troops tried to retake Quebec. Only 3,000 British soldiers defended the city. William and the troops he commanded were the first British soldiers to attack the 8,000 French soldiers as they approached

William led a daring assault on French troops in 1759 in the Battle of Quebec, Canada. His actions gave the British a major victory in the fight to control Canada.

the city. The following battle was costly to both sides. One thousand British and one thousand French soldiers were killed, wounded, or missing.

But because the British began the battle with many fewer troops than the French, they could not afford to lose so many soldiers. With the British troops greatly outnumbered, the French decided to lay siege to the city, preventing anyone from entering or leaving Quebec. The French hoped to force the British to surrender by cutting them off from supplies of food, water, clothes, and additional soldiers. But a large number of British troop reinforcements, brought by ship, soon arrived to help defeat the French, giving Great Britain a significant victory. In 1763, the French and British signed a peace treaty ending the war. Britain controlled all of Canada.

William, a war hero, was promoted to the rank of colonel. He was sent to Ireland, where he met and fell in love with Fannie Conolly. They married on June 4, 1765.

William became a major general in 1772. In 1774, he was given the important job of training British soldiers. Although the war against France was over, there was still trouble in North America. The French and Indian War had been very expensive. To help raise money to pay for the war, the British government passed laws taxing many products used by Americans, from stamps to tea.

Americans did not like these taxes and protested against them. Many Americans in the 13 colonies were angry about British rule over them. These Americans, called **Patriots**, protested against King

In 1774, William was given the job of training British soldiers. Men wearing British uniforms and carrying bayonets are shown here in this reenactment.

George III and wanted to govern themselves. Other Americans, called **Loyalists**, supported the king and wanted to continue to be ruled by Great Britain. By 1774, Patriots began to talk about a war of independence against the king.

Back in England, William was campaigning for reelection to Parliament in 1774. There was much concern that there would be a war between Britain and the American colonies. Most of the people of

Nottingham did not support war against America. They asked William what he would do if such a war began. William felt the same as most of his constituents. He told them that if war broke out between Great Britain and America, he would decline any offers to fight in that war. Satisfied with his answer, the people of Nottingham reelected him to Parliament.

William and the Howe family were very fond of Americans and the 13 colonies. William publicly criticized how King George's government treated the colonies. During the French and Indian War, many of the men who served in George Howe's various troops were from the colony of Massachusetts. One troop liked their commander so much that after his death in battle, the soldiers and the Massachusetts colony paid for a monument to him to be built in Westminster Abbey in London, England.

As expected, war between Great Britain and her colonies came in 1775. When the war began, King George III summoned William to appear at Buckingham Palace, the king's home in London. At that meeting, the king gave William command of a large number of British soldiers in America. Remembering what he had told his constituents in Nottingham about turning down any offer to fight the colonies, William asked the king if he was ordering him to fight in the war. King George III answered yes.

This was not an offer. This was a royal command. William left the palace knowing he could not refuse an order from the king. So, despite his warm feelings for America, William Howe began preparing to return to the New World, this time to fight against Great Britain's 13 colonies.

The 13 original American colonies were New Hampshire, Massachusetts, Connecticut, Rhode Island, New York, New Jersey, Delaware, Pennsylvania, Maryland, Virginia, North Carolina, South Carolina, and Georgia. In 1774, the Continental Congress, with representatives from 12 of the 13 colonies (Georgia did not participate at first), was formed to be the government of the people in the colonies. The Congress met in Philadelphia, Pennsylvania. In 1775, when the American Revolution was about to begin, Congress created the **Continental Army** to fight the British. On June 10, 1775, George Washington was given the rank of general and appointed commander in chief of the Continental Army. During the revolution, American soldiers were also sometimes called Continentals.

British Commanding General Thomas Gage was involved in the earliest fighting of the Revolutionary War in Lexington and Concord. William Howe received his orders from Gage to attack colonists on Bunker Hill.

The War Begins

1f you lived in Boston in April 1775, you knew that trouble was coming. British Commanding General Thomas Gage had a large army in the city. There were so many British soldiers, who were also called **redcoats** because of the garments they wore, that Gage had many stay in people's houses, instead of in army bases. This made many people in Boston angry. It also made the city look like a big army camp, with soldiers everywhere.

General Gage ordered his soldiers to march all around the Boston area. He wanted to show the Patriots how powerful the British army was. Gage believed that the colonists could never beat the British army, the world's strongest, in battle. He thought the people around Boston would think so too when they saw British soldiers, dressed in bright red coats and white pants, with sparkling **muskets**, marching through their towns. Gage also had his soldiers take weapons, ammunition, and supplies belonging to Americans that the soldiers found during their marches.

Seeing the British troops just made the colonists angrier. Patriots did not want to be told what to do anymore, by the British army or by King George III. They did not like having soldiers staying in their houses, eating their food, and taking their weapons.

On April 15, 1775, Patriot leaders in Boston learned that General Gage planned to send 700 soldiers outside of Boston to take more supplies away from colonists living in the small towns of Lexington and Concord. These leaders knew they had to warn the people in Lexington, Concord, and other towns that the British were coming. They asked Paul Revere, a well-known Boston Patriot, to ride his horse and warn the Patriots in the small towns.

Paul rode one of the fastest horses in Massachusetts to warn people about the British. All along the way to Lexington, in farmhouse after farmhouse, he woke people to give them the news. After hearing from Paul, they pulled on their clothes, grabbed their guns, and gathered to join the **minutemen**. Paul reached Lexington around midnight, and warned minutemen and Patriot leaders John Hancock and Sam Adams that the British were coming.

Although the British captured Paul for a short time on his way to Concord, he had done his job. Patriots were ready for the redcoats. As the 700 British soldiers marched toward Lexington, they had no idea people knew they were coming. Finally, the soldiers reached a

This man is dressed as a minuteman from colonial America. These patriots were called minutemen because they were ready to fight the British at a minute's notice.

small town square called the Lexington Green where they saw armed colonists. Both sides faced each other, weapons pointed and ready to shoot. No one is sure who it was, but someone fired his rifle. Then, several British soldiers fired. Smoke from the guns was everywhere.

As the smoke cleared, the colonists retreated from the town square. Eight Americans were dead. No British soldiers were hurt. The American Revolution had begun.

The British left Lexington and marched on to Concord. In Concord and outside of town, minutemen and other colonists waited for them. From behind almost every tree, fence, farmhouse and barn, colonists fired on the redcoats. Bullets whistled all around, as the British were hit from all sides. British soldiers fell to the ground in large numbers, and they started to retreat. The colonists kept firing, and the redcoats, who could not see where to shoot since the colonists were so well hidden, ran as fast as they could back to Boston. The Americans had won.

William arrived in Boston in May, after the

Armed patriots were waiting for the British soldiers to arrive in Lexington thanks to Paul Revere's warning. The fighting marked the beginning of the American Revolution.

battles of Lexington and Concord. By that time, American **militia** surrounded Boston and laid siege to the city. In June 1775, General Gage decided it was time to attack the Americans.

Gage ordered William to attack colonists who were on Breed's Hill, a large hill overlooking Boston harbor. The Americans prepared for the British invasion. They dug holes in the ground to hide in and built barricades to shoot from. These would give the soldiers protection against the British bullets.

In the early morning of June 17, four powerful British warships opened fire on Breed's Hill. Their cannons blasted the American positions, where about 1,500 militiamen hid, and waited for the British attack. The tremendous noise from the cannons seemed to shake the ground the Americans were standing on. As dozens of cannon balls flew above them, soldiers could hear tremendous whooshing sounds as they

Artemas Ward, senior general of the Massachusetts Army, ordered William Prescott to take his soldiers to Bunker Hill, another hill overlooking Boston harbor. He wanted them to fortify the hill, to prevent the British from capturing it. But Prescott made a mistake. Instead of Bunker Hill, he went up Breed's Hill. This is where William Howe and the British attacked. But the fighting there became known as the Battle of Bunker Hill, even though the battle was fought on Breed's Hill.

roared past. Smoke filled the air so it was hard to see.

When the British guns stopped firing, General Howe prepared to charge up Breed's Hill. At the bottom of the hill, he stood with about 2,300 soldiers, some of the finest in the British army. Before attacking, William spoke to his men and said, "Gentlemen, I am very happy in having the honor of commanding so fine a body of men. I do not have the least doubt that you will behave as Englishmen, and as becometh good soldiers."

After he finished speaking, William stood at the front of his soldiers and led them up Breed's Hill. The climb was hard. The soldiers had to march around trees, fences, and blackberry bushes. They also carried about 125 pounds of equipment on their backs, including blankets and food.

Finally, the British neared the top of the hill. When the soldiers were about 15 feet away from the Americans, the militia opened fire. The first

Bunker Hill was the site of a bloody battle between William's men and the American militia. The British won the battle, but many men died or were wounded.

rows of British soldiers fell to the ground. Other soldiers passed them, but American bullets hit them, too. Finally, after several tries, the British retreated down the hill.

Once again, William's men climbed the hill

and attacked. For about an hour, the British tried to defeat the militiamen. But again, the Americans forced them to retreat. At the bottom of Breed's Hill, about 400 British reinforcements met Howe and his soldiers. With these fresh troops, the British stormed up the hill for a third attack.

This time, the British were too much for the militia. The Americans ran out of ammunition, and the redcoats jumped over the holes and barricades the militia had built. General Howe won the battle. But many men had been hurt or killed. About half of the 2,300 British soldiers who attacked Breed's Hill were either dead or wounded, along with more than 400 Americans. After the battle, the British still controlled Boston. But the Americans controlled the countryside outside the city.

After receiving news about the battle, many people in England were angry that so many soldiers had been hurt or killed. They blamed General Gage for ordering the attack. King

George was so upset that he removed General Gage from his post and made William Howe the commander of British troops in America.

While many English people were unhappy about the Battle of Bunker Hill, the Americans felt differently. Their militia had almost beaten some of the best soldiers in the world. British soldiers had better weapons and better training than the Americans, but they still had trouble defeating them in battle. The Patriots believed they had a chance against the powerful British. Next, the Americans wanted to force the British to leave Boston.

For the next 10 months, during the summer, fall, and winter of 1775–1776, the Americans put cannons and soldiers on the hills all around Boston. By early March 1776, the Americans had the British completely surrounded. William knew he was trapped. Surrounded by American soldiers, he decided to leave Boston, rather than fight. He believed he had little chance to defeat the Americans in battle.

William ordered the British soldiers to evacuate Boston.
The soldiers boarded ships bound for Canada.

On March 17, 1776, William Howe ordered
British soldiers in the city to board ships waiting
in Boston harbor. After all British troops were on

board, the ships left Boston, and sailed for Halifax, a city in Canada. The redcoats were gone, and they never returned to Boston. The Americans had won a great victory.

Once William Howe arrived in Halifax, he needed to figure out what to do next. Not wanting to return to Boston, he thought about where else the British could attack the Americans.

The Battle of Long Island, New York, was a great victory for William. But Continental soldiers from Maryland and Delaware were able to maintain the fight long enough to allow the rest of George Washington's troops to escape the capture.

Victory in
New York

In Canada, William Howe planned his next move. With reinforcements arriving in Halifax from England, he decided to attack New York City. In June, after his army had rested in Canada, the British sailed south to New York. William's army arrived there on June 25, 1776, and landed on Staten Island, east of Manhattan. Other British ships and soldiers docked in New York almost every day for about a month after Howe's arrival. On June 29, Daniel McCurtin, who lived in a house near the harbor where the British landed, looked out his front window and could not believe what he saw. He wrote, ". . . [T]he whole Bay was as full of shipping as ever it could be. I . . . thought all London was afloat."

On July 12, William's brother, Admiral Richard Howe, arrived from England, with about 150 warships, carrying 10,000 British and 1,000 German soldiers, plus guns, ammunition, and other supplies. The German soldiers were **mercenaries**, who were paid by King George III to fight for Great Britain. Most of these men came from a part of Germany called Hesse, so the men were called Hessians.

Shortly after Richard Howe's arrival, two British generals with about 2,500 more soldiers arrived in New York from South Carolina. By the end of July 1776, William commanded an army of 32,000 soldiers. This was the largest British army ever gathered overseas to fight a war. William also had all the supplies he needed and a large fleet of warships. He was ready to fight the Americans.

Even before William left Canada, General George Washington tried to figure out where the

British would attack next. He correctly guessed that New York would be the place. So, while William was in Halifax, George Washington hurried to bring more American soldiers to New York. But his army was still much smaller than Howe's. Washington also did not have any warships; the British had more than 150.

But before the British attacked Washington, William and Richard Howe first tried to end the war peacefully. They both were still sympathetic to the Americans, and wished they did not have to fight them. At the British army head-quarters on Staten Island, Admiral Howe met with several Patriot leaders, including Benjamin Franklin and John Adams, to discuss peace. The British wanted to end the war but would not allow the Americans to become independent. But the Americans did not want to be subjects of King George anymore.

While these talks continued, the **Continental Congress** approved the Declaration of Independence on July 4, 1776. This document stated that

A public reading of the Declaration of Independence
is shown here. Thomas Jefferson, a young lawyer from
Virginia, wrote the document at the request of the
Continental Congress.

the Americans wished to be free of British rule,
and wanted their own, independent country.
The Declaration of Independence ended the
peace talks. The Howe brothers knew there
would be no peace now. They had no choice but
to fight the Americans.

On August 22, several British warships, carrying more than 15,000 soldiers, sailed from Staten Island. The troops landed at Gravesend Bay on Long Island. All day, British warships and transports sailed back and forth from Staten Island, with more soldiers and supplies. No American ships or guns could stop them. At about the same time, another 15,000 British and Hessian troops landed in Brooklyn, across the East River from Manhattan Island. The British were trying to surround the American army, most of which was on Long Island and in Brooklyn.

Early on the morning of August 25, the British attacked, and the Battle of Long Island began. At about the same time, 5,000 Hessians attacked the Americans in Brooklyn Heights.

The larger British army quickly overwhelmed the Americans, who retreated. Washington's army was in danger of being destroyed. To avoid a disastrous defeat, the American soldiers needed time to get away from the British. Continental soldiers from Maryland and Delaware fought hard on Long Island to keep the British from capturing other American troops before they could escape. Although the British defeated the Maryland and Delaware soldiers before the morning ended, the rest of the American army was able to get away.

By noon, the Battle of Long Island was over. William had won a great victory. More than 1,500 American soldiers had been killed, wounded, or captured. The Hessians also defeated the Americans at the Battle of Brooklyn Heights. The Continental Army had been badly beaten. But William was unable to capture or completely destroy the Americans. About 10,000 Continental soldiers remained in Brooklyn after the battles. George Washington, worried about another British attack, knew he needed to get his soldiers safely to Manhattan, across the East River and away from the enemy.

From August 28 to August 30, General Washington used small boats to escape to Manhattan,

George Washington retreated from Long Island and used small boats to cross the East River to Manhattan. Despite storms and darkness, the soldiers were able to escape to safety.

right past the British warships. At night on the 28th, the Americans rowed across the river. These soldiers were told to be as quiet as possible, so the enemy would not know what they were doing. A bad storm, with plenty of rain and wind, plus darkness made it difficult for the Americans to see where they were going. But the weather also made it hard for the British soldiers and sailors to see. The first group of Americans reached Manhattan safely. Washington ordered his men to row all night, and the next night too, to get as many soldiers as possible away from the British. It was not until about 4 P.M. on August 30, when there were very few Americans left in Brooklyn, that the British and Germans discovered what Washington had done. But it was too late. The American army had arrived safely in Manhattan.

Washington was still concerned about the British. He knew William and his soldiers would come after his army. General Washington needed to know what William's army was doing, so he could prepare for any attack. He asked one of his officers to send a spy to Long Island to learn the British plans. This spy was Nathan Hale, an American army captain from Connecticut. Before the war, Hale had been a teacher. When he reached Long Island, he pretended to be a schoolmaster. He even carried his college diploma, from Yale College in Connecticut, to try to fool the British into believing he was just a teacher.

Hale reached the British army base on Long Island in mid-September, while William Howe was planning to attack Manhattan. While the British were busy with their battle preparations, Nathan Hale tried to learn all he could about their plans. He took notes of what he saw, and kept them in his pockets.

On September 15, William sent his warships up the East and Hudson Rivers, which flow on both sides of Manhattan. When the ships were in position, he ordered them to bombard the city with their cannons. The noise and damage from British cannonballs terrified people living there as well as many of the American soldiers. As Howe's redcoats and Hessians landed in Manhattan, the American soldiers quickly retreated north. But the British were slow in following them. This was partly because a large fire destroyed most of Manhattan earlier in September. The British lost a lot of supplies in that fire, but still had plenty left, much more than Washington's soldiers. Soon, Howe had his soldiers chasing the Americans again.

Meanwhile, Nathan Hale was still on Long Island, gathering more information for General Washington. But on September 21, British soldiers captured him. They found the notes he had taken and accused him of being a spy. He was taken to Manhattan, where Hale admitted he was an American officer, spying for Washington. William ordered that Hale be executed. The next day, September 22, 1776, the British killed Hale for spying.

The British allowed Captain William Hull, an American from Connecticut, to watch Nathan Hale's execution. Captain Hull wrote what he saw that day. "Captain Hale entered: he was calm, and bore himself with gentle dignity. . . . He asked for writing materials. . . . he wrote two letters, one to his mother and one to a brother officer." Captain Hull also wrote in his diary the famous words that Nathan Hale said before he died, "I only regret that I have but one life to lose for my country." These patriotic words made Nathan Hale a hero, remembered and admired by Americans for his bravery.

American army captain, Nathan Hale is led to his execution on September 22, 1776. William ordered Nathan's execution after he admitted to spying for George Washington.

The retreating Americans stopped at a place called Harlem Heights on Manhattan Island. There, on high ground, General Washington planned to fight the British. After a brief battle, the Americans succeeded in stopping the British only for a short time. Washington continued retreating north until he reached White Plains, a city in what is today called Westchester County. On October 28, the British attacked again and defeated the Americans at the Battle of White Plains. Washington continued his retreat, wanting to get as far away from the British as possible.

Later, at the Battle of Fort Washington in November, the British won another big victory. William Howe captured the fort, plus about 3,000 American soldiers, 146 cannons, 2,800 muskets, and large amounts of ammunition. Shortly after this battle, the British crossed the Hudson River, and captured Fort Lee, New Jersey, where Howe's soldiers again took large amounts of guns and ammunition from the Americans. The Americans continued retreating, moving south through New Jersey, and by the end of 1776, the British were in complete control of New York City and the areas closest to it in New York and New Jersey.

William Howe's capture of New York was

very important. After the British defeat in Boston, the Americans were confident they could defeat their enemy. But with the British capture of New York, the American army was in trouble. The Americans had lost many soldiers and much equipment in battle. They faced a powerful enemy, who now controlled New York. As the winter of 1776 began, William started planning how he could defeat the Americans and end the war.

British ships are shown here on the coast of New Jersey. The British and Hessian soldiers were pursuing the Americans as they retreated from New York.

The Turning Point

During November and December 1776, William and several thousand British and Hessian soldiers continued to chase the retreating Americans south through New Jersey. William pushed the Continental Army first out of Newark and then out of New Brunswick, New Jersey.

The retreating American army was falling apart. Soldiers had few supplies. They also had little warm clothing to protect them from the winter cold. After capturing several American troops, one British officer wrote that many of George Washington's men, "were without shoes or Stockings. . . or proper shirt. . . they must suffer extremely."

The retreating Americans finally reached the Delaware River in southern New Jersey. There, they boarded small boats, and rowed across the river to safety in Pennsylvania, where they rested. With the Americans in Pennsylvania, William stopped his chase, just a few days before Christmas 1776. He believed the war would soon be over. William and most of his army went back to New York. Small groups of British and Hessian soldiers were left behind to guard several New Jersey towns.

One of these towns was Trenton, where about 1,000 Hessians were stationed. On December 25 the Hessians celebrated Christmas and their victories over the Americans. They believed the war was almost over, and this Christmas would be their last in America.

At the same time, George Washington, knowing the Hessians did not expect an attack, decided to surprise the enemy. He gathered many small boats and led his soldiers quietly back across the Delaware to New Jersey. Washington told his men to make as

Washington's troops had to endure freezing conditions as they crossed the Delaware River from Pennsylvania to Trenton, New Jersey.

little noise as possible, so the Hessians would not discover they were returning to New Jersey.

The trip across the river was difficult. The Americans and General Washington pushed their boats through cold temperatures, sleet, and freezing rain, past big chunks of ice that were floating in the river.

They finally landed near Trenton. The Hessians still did not know the Americans were there. As the Hessians were asleep in their tents, Washington prepared his soldiers for battle early the next morning. At dawn, the Americans attacked and caught the enemy by surprise.

The Battle of Trenton was an unexpected American victory that made William change his decision not to chase the Americans. He sent about 8,000 soldiers, under the command of General Earl Charles Cornwallis, from New York to attack Washington's army of nearly 5,000 men.

Cornwallis quickly reached Trenton, where Washington's army was camped. The British general planned to trap the small American army and stop Washington from escaping. With the British surrounding him near Trenton, Washington knew he was outnumbered and could not defeat the larger enemy army.

So he decided to escape by taking his men back across the Delaware River to Pennsylvania. But to do this, he needed to fool Cornwallis into believing the Americans were asleep and not going anywhere. During the night of January 3, 1777, Washington had a small group of his soldiers keep the campfires lit in the camp, while the rest of the Continentals retreated to Pennsylvania. They did this all night, and Cornwallis, whose soldiers watched the American base that night, believed the Continentals would be there for him to attack the next morning.

That morning, Cornwallis discovered he had been tricked. Washington and the Americans had escaped from the British again and camped near Philadelphia, Pennsylvania, for the winter. General Cornwallis returned to New York, where most of the British army camped for the winter. The fighting was over until springtime.

While the Americans had little to eat and few warm clothes and blankets at their winter base, William and his soldiers enjoyed staying in warm houses, with plenty of food in New York City. There, the British commander thought about where to attack when the warm weather came.

William was also rewarded for capturing New York. King George III gave him a medal, called the Order of the Bath. In January 1777, the medal arrived by ship from England. Richard Howe pinned the medal on his brother in a celebration of the British victory in New York.

As the winter continued, William decided to attack Philadelphia next. The city was the capital of the Americans' new hoped for country, the United States. Capturing the enemy capital would be very important and could end the war.

On July 23, 1777, Howe began preparing to move his army from New York. But first, he had to decide whether to attack Philadelphia by sea or by land. He decided to leave 7,000 soldiers to guard New York City and put several thousand more British soldiers onto 45 transport ships. These ships, guarded by 16 warships, sailed south from New York to the Chesapeake Bay. Once they reached the bay, the British fleet sailed north. The troops landed near Elkton, Maryland, on August 25 and marched about 50 miles north toward Philadelphia.

The trip south to the bay and then north to Philadelphia took about one month to complete. This long voyage gave the American army, which had learned about Howe's plans the day he left New York City, time to prepare for the British attack.

While William sailed to Philadelphia, two other British armies prepared to attack the Americans north of New York City. One army of British and Hessian soldiers, commanded by General John Burgoyne, marched south from Canada. A smaller army, with British, Hessian, Native American, and Loyalist troops, commanded by Colonel Barry St. Leger, marched east. They planned to meet near Albany, New York, about 180 miles north of New York City, and then attack American soldiers there. The British wanted to chase the Americans out of New York, and attack New England, possibly even Boston. If the British were successful, King George's soldiers would control a very large area.

But there was confusion about this plan. General Burgoyne and Colonel St. Leger expected William to sail north up the Hudson River from New York,

British General John Burgoyne marched his men south from Canada to New York. The plan was to meet William's troops in Albany. In fact, William was heading south to Philadelphia instead of to meet Burgoyne.

and meet them in Albany. These officers did not know that instead of coming to meet them, William was sailing to Philadelphia. At the time, Howe said he never received any orders from England to sail to Albany. Some historians think he decided by himself to attack Philadelphia, rather than join the two British armies in northern New York. Others believe William received orders from England after he had begun his voyage to Philadelphia, too late to help Burgoyne and St. Leger.

As William's 12,000 soldiers headed to Philadelphia, the Continental Army and General Washington marched south from near Monmouth, New Jersey, and went through Philadelphia, where crowds cheered the soldiers on their way to fight the British.

About 20 miles southwest of Philadelphia, the American army stopped at a small creek called the Brandywine. Washington thought this was the best place to meet the enemy in

Even though they were on opposite sides, William and George Washington still respected each other. During the Battle of Germantown, William somehow lost his dog. He did not know where the dog was, or if it was even still alive. William was worried, but on October 6, he received a letter with good news from General Washington. The letter said: "General Washington's compliments to General Howe. He does himself the pleasure to return him a dog, which accidentally fell into his hands, and by the inscription on the Collar, appears to belong to General Howe."

battle. He put most of his 15,000 soldiers on top of cliffs, on both sides of the creek. This spot, Washington believed, with his soldiers shooting their rifles downhill against the British, was the best place to defend Philadelphia.

When William reached Brandywine Creek and was near the Continental Army, he decided to divide his 12,000-man army. Half of his soldiers would try to fool the Americans into believing they would attack a place called Chadds Ford, where some American soldiers were stationed, instead of Brandy-wine Creek. Chadds Ford is located a few miles away from the Brandywine. The other half of William's army marched several miles behind Washington's men, who were stationed at Brandywine Creek, and then planned to attack from the rear.

On September 11, 1777, the Battle of Brandy-wine began. The Americans were surprised by the British attack from behind. Washington ordered his army to retreat, and his soldiers fled north. The battle ended when it became too dark for the armies to fight anymore. A heavy rainstorm also damaged the Americans' ammunition, so they had no bullets and powder to fight the British.

With the Americans retreating, William led his army into Philadelphia. The American Continental Congress, not wanting to be captured by the British, fled from the city to the small town of Lancaster, west of Philadelphia.

After the Battle of Brandywine, William moved 9,000 soldiers north of Philadelphia and set up camp in Germantown, Pennsylvania. Here, the British stayed in many of the town's houses. William did not expect Washington to attack. He thought the Americans, soundly beaten at Brandywine Creek, were in no condition to fight again anytime soon.

But the Americans quickly surprised the British. On October 3 and 4, Washington moved his soldiers toward Germantown. He divided the army into four groups. Each group was supposed to attack a different part of the British position.

But bad luck spoiled this plan. When the Americans attacked Germantown on October 4, the British were surprised, and they quickly retreated. However, heavy fog soon prevented the Americans from seeing where the redcoats were. The British made things worse by setting several haystacks on fire. The fog and smoke from the fires confused the attacking Americans. They could not see the enemy or each other. Some Americans accidentally fired at their own soldiers.

As the British retreated, some soldiers stopped at an old house, with thick walls of gray stone, which belonged to Pennsylvania Chief Justice Benjamin Chew. Here, about 120 redcoats fought the Americans. For about an hour, the armies battled back and forth. The Americans tried to blast the British out of the house. But American cannon-balls just bounced off the house's thick stonewalls. Soon, other British soldiers moved toward the Continentals. The heavy fog and the large numbers of advancing British soldiers forced the Americans to retreat. The Battle of Germantown was another great victory for William and the British. The American army, which had more than 1,000

The British and Americans continued the fighting from the Battle of Germantown at this house, which was owned by Pennsylvania Chief Justice Benjamin Chew.

casualties in the Battles of Brandywine and Germantown, was in poor shape. Many soldiers were hurt, and a large amount of equipment had been lost in battle. If the British chased them, the Americans might have lost again. But William decided not to attack and instead returned to Philadelphia.

General Burgoyne is shown here surrendering after the Battle of Saratoga, New York.

Criticism
from Britain

oyalists in Philadelphia, who supported King
George, were very happy the British were
defeating the Americans. Once again, William was
congratulated for his victories. Loyalists held many
celebrations and parties for William and his soldiers.

But while the British were enjoying these celebrations in the American capital, William soon received
bad news from New York. On October 17, 1777, the
British were defeated at the Battle of Saratoga, which
took place north of Albany, New York. The Americans captured more than 5,000 British soldiers in the
battle. This was an embarrassing defeat for the

British. Now, the Americans controlled all of northern New York. They could even invade Canada and attack the British there. They could also attack New York City. This victory also showed the world that the Americans could defeat the British in a large, important battle.

For the rest of October and November, William attacked American forts on the Delaware River. These strong forts, with many cannons, blocked the British from sending supplies on the Delaware River to Philadelphia. But William, helped by British warships commanded by his brother Richard, drove the Americans out of these forts. Washington's army, defeated, hungry, and with few supplies, retreated again, and moved into winter camp at Valley Forge, west of Philadelphia. The Americans were starving and freezing. With almost no food, tattered uniforms, and hardly any warm clothes, Washington's army prepared for its most difficult winter of the war. The British returned to Philadelphia where they would spend a warm winter, safe in the

George Washington's army spent the winter of 1777 at Valley Forge, which is west of Philadelphia. There was almost no food or other supplies. Most soldiers lived in tents and were soaked by the icy rain and snow.

city's houses with plenty to eat and drink.

Many people in England were angry about the defeat of General Burgoyne and Colonel St. Leger at Saratoga. They blamed William because he decided to attack Philadelphia, instead of helping General Burgoyne in New York. William was criticized for not attacking the Americans after their Brandywine and Germantown defeats, when they were weakest. He was also further blamed for letting the American army escape many times, from Long Island, Brooklyn, and Germantown. His opponents also thought William should attack the weak American army at Valley Forge, instead of staying in Philadelphia.

William was upset by this criticism. He believed he had done well as the British commander in America, winning many victories, and capturing New York City and Philadelphia. But he was homesick for England, and had grown tired of fighting in America. Several weeks before the Battle of Germantown, he asked to be replaced as the British commander. On February 4, 1778, King George granted his request.

While William prepared to return home, the Americans received some very good news. On February 6, 1778, France and the United States of America signed a treaty of **alliance** against Great Britain. This treaty meant that the French, with a powerful army and navy, would help fight the British. The treaty also said that there would be no peace agreement unless America became an independent country. The Continental Army's victory at Saratoga convinced the French to become America's ally. France now believed that the United States could defeat Great Britain.

In early May, William's replacement, General Henry Clinton, arrived from England.

But before William sailed back home, he was given a large going away party in New York. More than 400 people said goodbye to the general at this party. There was dancing and plenty of fancy food. Boats with colorful decorations, with William in the largest boat, filled New York harbor. The party ended at dawn with a tremendous fireworks display. On May 24, William boarded a British warship and sailed to England.

George Washington (left) rides into battle in Monmouth, New Jersey. The Continentals fought the British in sweltering weather and forced the British to retreat.

A Soldier's End

After William left America, both sides prepared to fight again. General Clinton and his men decided to leave Philadelphia and march to New York City, through New Jersey, instead of going by ship. General Washington, after learning about these plans, decided to attack the British army before it reached New York.

The hot June weather made the march difficult for the British. Temperatures were about 100 degrees, and the British soldiers wore heavy wool uniforms. They also carried more than 75 pounds of equipment on their backs. Many British troops died from the heat on their way through New Jersey.

The American army was stronger and larger than it had been during the winter. With help from the French, the soldiers now had plenty of food, ammunition, and equipment. The American army was also better trained than at any other time in the war.

Baron Friedrich Wilhelm von Steuben, a Prussian officer helping the Americans, trained the Continental Army at Valley Forge during the winter and made them into good soldiers.

In June 1778, at the Battle of Monmouth in New Jersey, the Americans forced General Clinton and his men to retreat to New York. The Americans considered this to be a victory. This battle showed how successful von Steuben's training had

John Hays from Pennsylvania fought against the British at the Battle of Monmouth. He was a gunner, responsible for firing one of the Continental Army's cannons. During the battle, his wife, Mary Hays, was with him. She brought water to the American soldiers, who were thirsty because of the hot temperatures and the heat from their cannons. At one point, John was wounded, taken off the battlefield, and replaced by Mary. She stood by the cannon during the battle, firing at the British soldiers. Later, she became known as Molly Pitcher, named for the pitchers of water she carried to the American soldiers.

Baron Von Steuben is shown here training the American army at Valley Forge.

been at Valley Forge. The new American army, disciplined and ready to fight, would be difficult for the British to defeat.

Now in England, William returned to the House of Commons in Parliament where he still represented Nottingham. He gave many speeches in Parliament, telling others about his experiences in America and his opinions of the war. But many English people still criticized some of the decisions William made while fighting in America. William's opponents also said that because he never supported war against the 13 colonies, he did not do his best to defeat the Americans. They believed he had been a poor commander.

In early 1779, William and his brother Richard were upset about this continued criticism. They wanted to clear William's name, so they asked Parliament to investigate General Howe's conduct during the war.

This investigation began in the spring of 1779. Many witnesses appeared in Parliament and gave their opinions about William's conduct in America. On April 22, 1779, William himself stood before Parliament to testify about how well he performed his job as British commander. He believed strongly that he had done his best. William defended himself against all the criticism, telling Parliament that he had been unjustly accused of being a poor general.

Despite listening to many witnesses and reviewing hundreds of documents, Parliament chose not to make any decision about William. On June 29, 1779, Parliament ended the investigation. William believed this would also end all criticism about his career in America. After all, King George still thought he had been a good commander and did not forget William's many victories in the colonies.

Meanwhile, the war in America was not going well for the British. In 1779, Spain, another powerful European country, joined France in fighting against Great Britain. In October 1781, the Americans and French fought the British at the Battle of Yorktown in Virginia. The combined forces defeated the British army commanded by General Cornwallis. On October 19, 1781, more than 8,000 British soldiers surrendered. This was the last major battle of the war. Peace negotiations began in Paris shortly after the battle. On September 3, 1783, the Treaty of Paris was signed, and the

The Battle of Yorktown was a decisive victory for the combined American-French army. The defeat of General Cornwallis's army forced the British government to seek terms of peace.

war was officially over. By December the British had left the 13 colonies and recognized a new country, the United States of America. The Americans had won their independence.

After the war was over, King George gave William new assignments. In 1782, he was named the general in charge of the army's weapons department. In 1793, William was promoted to the rank of full general. When his brother Richard died in 1799, William became the fifth Viscount Howe. Being a viscount was a great honor for William, who in 1805 was also appointed governor-general of Portsmouth, an important port city in England. Being governor-general of Portsmouth meant William was the official in charge of the port.

On July 12, 1814, William Howe died after a long illness. He was 85 years old. Living to that age in the early 19th century was very unusual. William was considered to be an excellent general, who helped win some of the most important battles of the French and Indian War and the American Revolution. Although he was criticized for letting the American army escape in several battles, William Howe was still the most successful British general during the American War of Independence.

GLOSSARY

alliance–when two or more countries are friendly, agree to help each other, and fight against common enemies.

casualties–soldiers who are killed, wounded or missing in battle.

Continental Congress–legislature of the American colonists.

Continental Army–another name for the American army during the revolution.

dragoons–a unit of horse soldiers in the British army.

French and Indian War–war between France and Great Britain over control of North America, which lasted from 1754-1763, and was won by Great Britain; also called the Seven Years' War.

general–highest-ranking officer in the army.

Hessians–Soldiers from Hesse, a part of Germany.

Loyalists–Americans who supported King George III, opposed the American War of Independence, and wanted to remain part of Great Britain.

mercenaries–soldiers paid by one side in a war to fight for that side.

militia–a group of civilians who become soldiers in emergencies.

minutemen–men who were ready to fight at a minute's notice.

musket–a type of rifle.

Parliament–the government of Great Britain.

Patriots–Americans who protested against the rule of King George III, and wanted independence from Great Britain.

redcoats–nickname given to British soldiers because of the red coats they wore.

regiment–a military unit of soldiers, usually commanded by a colonel.

viscount–a title held by some English noblemen.

CHRONOLOGY

1729	William Howe is born in England on August 10.
1746	Begins military career in the Duke of Cumberland's Light Dragoons.
1758	Becomes member of Parliament and sails to America to fight in the French and Indian War.
1759	Helps General Wolfe defeat the French in the Battle of Quebec.
1772	Promoted to major general.
1775	Given command of a large number of British soldiers in America by King George III and defeats Continental Army at the Battle of Bunker Hill.
1776	Defeats American army in several battles in New York and executes Nathan Hale as an American spy.
1777	Defeats American army at Battles of Brandywine Creek and Germantown and occupies Philadelphia.
1778	King George replaces Howe as British commander in America, and he returns to England.
1781	United States and France defeat British army at Battle of Yorktown, ending the American War of Independence.
1783	Great Britain and the United States sign treaty making the former 13 colonies an independent country.
1793	Rises to the rank of full general.
1799	Becomes fifth Viscount Howe.
1814	Dies in England on July 12 at the age of 85.

REVOLUTIONARY WAR TIME LINE ⸺

1765   The Stamp Act is passed by the British. Violent protests against it break out in the colonies.

1766   Britain ends the Stamp Act.

1767   Britain passes a law that taxes glass, painter's lead, paper, and tea in the colonies.

1770   Five colonists are killed by British soldiers in the Boston Massacre.

1773   People are angry about the taxes on tea. They throw boxes of tea from ships in Boston harbor into the water. It ruins the tea. The event is called the Boston Tea Party.

1774   The British pass laws to punish Boston for the Boston Tea Party. They close Boston harbor. Leaders in the colonies meet to plan a response to these actions.

1775   The battles of Lexington and Concord begin the American Revolution.

1776   The Declaration of Independence is signed. France and Spain give money to help the Americans fight Britain. Nathan Hale is captured by the British. He is charged with being a spy and is executed.

1777   Leaders choose a flag for America. The American troops win some important battles over the British. General Washington and his troops spend a very cold, hungry winter in Valley Forge.

1778   France sends ships to help the Americans win the war. The British are forced to leave Philadelphia.

1779	French ships head back to France. The French support the Americans in other ways.
1780	Americans discover that Benedict Arnold is a traitor. He escapes to the British. Major battles take place in North and South Carolina.
1781	The British surrender at Yorktown.
1783	A peace treaty is signed in France. British troops leave New York.
1787	The U.S. Constitution is written. Delaware becomes the first state in the Union.
1789	George Washington becomes the first president. John Adams is vice president.

FURTHER READING

Barner, Bob. *Which Way to the Revolution?* A Book About Maps. New York: Holiday House, 1998.

Bliven, Bruce. *American Revolution.* New York: Random House, 1987.

Draper, Allison Stark. *What People Wore During the American Revolution.* New York: PowerKids Press, 2000.

Moore, Kay. *If You Lived at the Time of the American Revolution.* New York: Scholastic, 1998.

Quackenbush, Robert M. *Daughter of Liberty – A True Story of the American Revolution.* New York: Hyperion, 1999.

PICTURE CREDITS

INDEX

ABOUT THE AUTHOR

BRUCE ADELSON has written 12 books for adults and children, including *Brushing Back Jim Crow–The Integration of Minor League Baseball in the American South* and *The Composite Guide to Field Hockey,* as well as three other historical biographies for children. A former elementary school substitute teacher and former commentator for National Public Radio and CBS Radio, Bruce is currently a book/multimedia reviewer for Children's Literature, a practicing attorney, and the proud father of Michael Daniel who was born in April 2001.

Senior Consulting Editor **ARTHUR M. SCHLESINGER, JR.** is the leading American historian of our time. He won the Pulitzer Prize for his book *The Age of Jackson* (1945), and again for *A Thousand Days* (1965). This chronicle of the Kennedy Administration also won a National Book Award. He has written many other books, including a multi-volume series, *The Age of Roosevelt.* Professor Schlesinger is the Albert Schweitzer Professor of the Humanities at the City University of New York, and has been involved in several other Chelsea House projects, including the Colonial Leaders series of biographies on the most prominent figures of early American history.

DEDICATION

This book is dedicated to Michael Daniel Adelson, who was born as this book was being complete. May your life be filled with joy, love, and many, many books.